# THE LOVE POEMS OF WILLIAM SHAKESPEARE

D0681122

Troll

ISBN 0-8167-7222-3

Printed in the United States of America.

10 9 8 7 6 5 4 3 2

PLAYS

f music be the food of love, play on;

Give me excess of it, that, surfeiting,

The appetite may sicken, and so die.

That strain again! it had a dying fall;

O, it came o'er my ear like the sweet sound

That breathes upon a bank of violets,

Stealing and giving odour!

*Twelfth Night* (I, i)

O she doth teach the torches to burn bright!
It seems she hangs upon the cheek of night
Like a rich jewel in an Ethiop's ear;
Beauty too rich for use, for earth too dear!
So shows a snowy dove trooping with crows,
As yonder lady o'er her fellows shows.
The measure done, I'll watch her place of stand,
And, touching hers, make blessed my rude hand.
Did my heart love till now? forswear it, sight!
For I ne'er saw true beauty till this night.

*Romeo and Juliet* (I, v)

ut, soft! what light through yonder
window breaks?

It is the east, and Juliet is the sun!

Arise, fair sun, and kill the envious moon,

Who is already sick and pale with grief

That thou her maid art far more fair than she.

Be not her maid, since she is envious;

Her vestal livery is but sick and green,

And none but fools do wear it; cast it off.

It is my lady; O, it is my love!

O, that she knew she were!

She speaks, yet she says nothing: what of that?

Her eye discourses; I will answer it.

I am too bold, 'tis not to me she speaks.

Two of the fairest stars in all the heaven,

Having some business, do entreat her eyes

To twinkle in their spheres till they return.

What if her eyes were there, they in her head?

The brightness of her cheek would shame those stars,

As daylight doth a lamp; her eyes in heaven

Would through the airy region stream so bright

That birds would sing and think it were not night.

See, how she leans her cheek upon her hand!

O, that I were a glove upon that hand,

That I might touch that cheek!

*Romeo and Juliet* (II, ii)

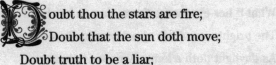

Doubt thou the stars are fire;
Doubt that the sun doth move;
Doubt truth to be a liar;
But never doubt I love.

*Hamlet* (II, ii)

Men are April when they woo, December when they wed. Maids are May when they are maids, but the sky changes when they are wives. I will be more jealous of thee than a Barbary cock-pigeon over his hen, more clamorous than a parrot against rain, more newfangled than an ape, more giddy in my desires than a monkey. I will weep for nothing, like Diana in the fountain, and I will do that when you are disposed to be merry; I will laugh like a hyen, and that when thou art inclined to sleep.

*As You Like It* (IV, i)

allop apace, you fiery-footed steeds,
Towards Phoebus' lodging: such a wagoner
As Phaethon would whip you to the west
And bring in cloudy night immediately.
Spread thy close curtain, love-performing night,
That runaways' eyes may wink and Romeo
Leap to these arms, untalked of and unseen.
Lovers can see to do their amorous rites
By their own beauties; or, if love be blind,
It best agrees with night. Come, civil night,
Thou sober-suited matron, all in black,
And learn me how to lose a winning match,
Played for a pair of stainless maidenhoods:
Hood my unmanned blood, bating in my cheeks,
With thy black mantle, till strange love, grown bold,
Think true love acted simple modesty.

Come, night; come, Romeo; come, thou day in night;

For thou wilt lie upon the wings of night

Whiter than new snow on a raven's back.

Come, gentle night, come, loving, black-browed night,

Give me my Romeo; and, when he shall die,

Take him and cut him out in little stars,

And he will make the face of heaven so fine

That all the world will be in love with night

And pay no worship to the garish sun.

O, I have bought the mansion of a love

But not possessed it, and, though I am sold,

Not yet enjoyed. So tedious is this day

As is the night before some festival

To an impatient child that hath new robes

And may not wear them.

### *Romeo and Juliet* (III, ii)

Cressid, I love thee in so strained a purity,

That the blest gods, as angry with my fancy,

More bright in zeal than the devotion which

Cold lips blow to their deities, take thee from me.

*Troilus and Cressida* (IV, iv)

Call thyself sister, sweet, for I am thee.
Thee will I love, and with thee lead my life;
Thou hast no husband yet, nor I no wife.
Give me thy hand.

*The Comedy of Errors* (III, ii)

To die is to be banished from myself;
And Silvia is myself: banished from her
Is self from self, a deadly banishment!
What light is light, if Silvia be not seen?
What joy is joy, if Silvia be not by?
Unless it be to think that she is by,
And feed upon the shadow of perfection.
Except I be by Silvia in the night,
There is no music in the nightingale;
Unless I look on Silvia in the day,
There is no day for me to look upon.
She is my essence, and I leave to be,
If I be not by her fair influence
Fostered, illumined, cherished, kept alive.
I fly not death, to fly his deadly doom:
Tarry I here, I but attend on death,
But, fly I hence, I fly away from life.

*The Two Gentlemen of Verona* (III, i)

O, take the sense, sweet, of my innocence!
Love takes the meaning in love's conference.
I mean that my heart unto yours is knit,
So that but one heart we can make of it:
Two bosoms interchained with an oath;
So then two bosoms and a single troth.
Then by your side no bed-room me deny;
For lying so, Hermia, I do not lie.

*A Midsummer Night's Dream* (II, ii)

f the scorn of your bright eyne

Have power to raise such love in mine,

Alack, in me what strange effect

Would they work in mild aspect!

Whiles you chid me, I did love;

How then might your prayers move!

He that brings this love to thee

Little knows this love in me;

And by him seal up thy mind,

Whether that thy youth and kind

Will the faithful offer take

Of me and all that I can make,

Or else by him my love deny,

And then I'll study how to die.

*As You Like It* (IV, iii)

There is my hand.
   A sister I bequeath you, whom no brother
Did ever love so dearly: let her live
To join our kingdoms and our hearts; and never
Fly off our loves again!

*Antony and Cleopatra* (II, ii)

'were all one
That I should love a bright particular star
And think to wed it, he is so above me.
In his bright radiance and collateral light
Must I be comforted, not in his sphere.
The ambition in my love thus plagues itself:
The hind that would be mated by the lion
Must die for love. 'Twas pretty, though a plague,
To see him every hour; to sit and draw
His arched brows, his hawking eye, his curls,
In our heart's table — heart too capable
Of every line and trick of his sweet favour.
But now he's gone, and my idolatrous fancy
Must sanctify his reliques.

*All's Well That Ends Well* (I, i)

O dear Ophelia,
I am ill at these numbers.
I have not art to reckon my groans,
but that I love thee best,
O most best, believe it.
Adieu.

*Hamlet* (II, ii)

My bounty is as boundless as the sea,
My love as deep; the more I give to thee,
The more I have, for both are infinite.

*Romeo and Juliet* (II, ii)

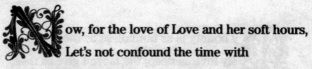 ow, for the love of Love and her soft hours,
Let's not confound the time with
conference harsh:
There's not a minute of our lives should stretch
Without some pleasure now. What sport tonight?

*Antony and Cleopatra* (I, i)

And, Benedick, love on; I will requite thee,
Taming my wild heart to thy loving hand.
If thou dost love, my kindness shall incite thee
To bind our loves up in a holy band;
For others say thou dost deserve, and I
Believe it better than reportingly.

*Much Ado About Nothing* (III, i)

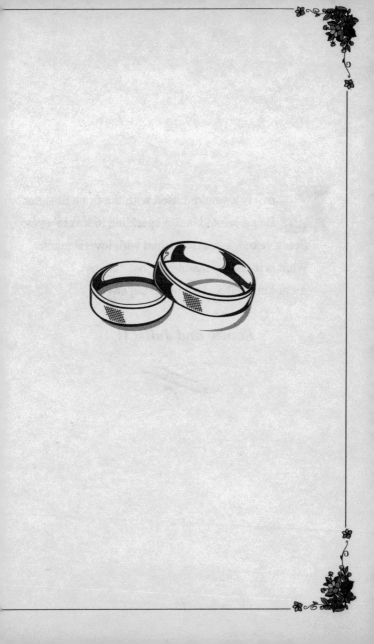

Love is a smoke raised with the fume of sighs;

Being purged, a fire sparkling in lovers' eyes;

Being vexed, a sea nourished with lovers' tears:

What is it else? a madness most discreet,

A choking gall and a preserving sweet.

*Romeo and Juliet* (I, i)

O heaven, O earth, bear witness to this sound,
And crown what I profess with kind event
If I speak true! if hollowly, invert
What best is boded me to mischief! I,
Beyond all limit of what else i' the world,
Do love, prize, honour you.

*The Tempest* (III, i)

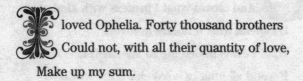

loved Ophelia. Forty thousand brothers
Could not, with all their quantity of love,
Make up my sum.

*Hamlet* (V, i)

'Tis but thy name that is my enemy;

Thou art thyself, though not a Montague.

What's Montague? it is nor hand, nor foot,

Nor arm, nor face, nor any other part

Belonging to a man. O, be some other name!

What's in a name? that which we call a rose

By any other name would smell as sweet;

So Romeo would, were he not Romeo called,

Retain that dear perfection which he owes

Without that title. Romeo, doff thy name,

And for that name, which is no part of thee,

Take all myself.

*Romeo and Juliet* (II, ii)

Then I confess,
Here on my knee, before high heaven and you,
That before you, and next unto high heaven,
I love your son.
My friends were poor, but honest; so's my love.
Be not offended; for it hurts not him
That he is loved of me: I follow him not
By any token of presumptuous suit;
Nor would I have him till I do deserve him;
Yet never know how that desert should be.
I know I love in vain, strive against hope;
Yet in this captious and intenible sieve
I still pour in the waters of my love
And lack not to lose still. Thus, Indian-like,
Religious in mine error, I adore
The sun that looks upon his worshipper

But knows of him no more. My dearest madam,

Let not your hate encounter with my love

For loving where you do; but if yourself,

Whose aged honour cites a virtuous youth,

Did ever in so true a flame of liking

Wish chastely and love dearly, that your Dian

Was both herself and love, O, then, give pity

To her whose state is such that cannot choose

But lend and give where she is sure to lose;

That seeks not to find that her search implies,

But, riddle-like, lives sweetly where she dies!

*All's Well That Ends Well* (I, iii)

SONNETS

# SONNET XVIII

Shall I compare thee to a summer's day?

Thou art more lovely and more temperate.

Rough winds do shake the darling buds of May,

And summer's lease hath all too short a date.

Sometime too hot the eye of heaven shines,

And often is his gold complexion dimmed;

And every fair from fair sometime declines,

By chance or nature's changing course untrimmed:

But thy eternal summer shall not fade,

Nor lose possession of that fair thou owest;

Nor shall Death brag thou wander'st in his shade,

When in eternal lines to time thou grow'st.

   So long as men can breathe or eyes can see,

   So long lives this, and this gives life to thee.

# Sonnet XXIII

As an unperfect actor on the stage,
Who with his fear is put besides his part,
Or some fierce thing replete with too much rage,
Whose strength's abundance weakens his own heart;
So I, for fear of trust, forget to say
The perfect ceremony of love's rite,
And in mine own love's strength seem to decay,
O'ercharged with burden of mine own love's might.
O, let my books be then the eloquence
And dumb presagers of my speaking breast,
Who plead for love, and look for recompense,
More than that tongue that more hath more expressed.
  O, learn to read what silent love hath writ:
  To hear with eyes belongs to love's fine wit.

# SONNET XXIV

Mine eye hath played the painter and hath stelled
Thy beauty's form in table of my heart;
My body is the frame wherein 'tis held,
And perspective it is best painter's art.
For through the painter must you see his skill,
To find where your true image pictured lies,
Which in my bosom's shop is hanging still,
That hath his windows glazed with thine eyes.
Now see what good turns eyes for eyes have done:
Mine eyes have drawn thy shape, and thine for me
Are windows to my breast, wherethrough the sun
Delights to peep, to gaze therein on thee.

   Yet eyes this cunning want to grace their art;
    They draw but what they see, know not the heart.

# SONNET XXV

Let those who are in favour with their stars
Of public honour and proud titles boast,
Whilst I, whom fortune of such triumph bars,
Unlooked for joy in that I honour most.
Great princes' favourites their fair leaves spread
But as the marigold at the sun's eye,
And in themselves their pride lies buried,
For at a frown they in their glory die.
The painful warrior famoused for fight,
After a thousand victories once foiled,
Is from the book of honour razed quite,
And all the rest forgot for which he toiled.
    Then happy I, that love and am beloved
    Where I may not remove nor be removed.

#  SONNET XXIX

When, in disgrace with fortune and men's eyes,

I all alone beweep my outcast state,

And trouble deaf heaven with my bootless cries,

And look upon myself and curse my fate,

Wishing me like to one more rich in hope,

Featured like him, like him with friends possessed,

Desiring this man's art and that man's scope,

With what I most enjoy contented least;

Yet in these thoughts myself almost despising,

Haply I think on thee, and then my state,

Like to the lark at break of day arising

From sullen earth, sings hymns at heaven's gate;

    For thy sweet love remembered such wealth brings

    That then I scorn to change my state with kings.

# SONNET XL

Take all my loves, my love, yea, take them all;

What hast thou then more than thou hadst before?

No love, my love, that thou mayst true love call;

All mine was thine before thou hadst this more.

Then, if for my love thou my love receivest,

I cannot blame thee for my love thou usest;

But yet be blamed, if thou thyself deceivest

By wilful taste of what thyself refusest.

I do forgive thy robbery, gentle thief,

Although thou steal thee all my poverty;

And yet, love knows, it is a greater grief

To bear love's wrong than hate's known injury.

    Lascivious grace, in whom all ill well shows,

    Kill me with spites; yet we must not be foes.

# SONNET XLVI

Mine eye and heart are at a mortal war

How to divide the conquest of thy sight;

Mine eye my heart thy picture's sight would bar,

My heart mine eye the freedom of that right.

My heart doth plead that thou in him dost lie,

A closet never pierced with crystal eyes;

But the defendant doth that plea deny

And says in him thy fair appearance lies.

To 'cide this title is impanelled

A quest of thoughts, all tenants to the heart;

And by their verdict is determined

The clear eye's moiety and the dear heart's part:

As thus: mine eye's due is thine outward part,

And my heart's right thine inward love of heart.

# SONNET XLIX

Against that time, if ever that time come,

When I shall see thee frown on my defects,

Whenas thy love hath cast his utmost sum,

Called to that audit by advised respects;

Against that time when thou shalt strangely pass

And scarcely greet me with that sun, thine eye,

When love, converted from the thing it was,

Shall reasons find of settled gravity;

Against that time do I ensconce me here

Within the knowledge of mine own desert,

And this my hand against myself uprear

To guard the lawful reasons on thy part.

   To leave poor me thou hast the strength of laws,

   Since why to love I can allege no cause.

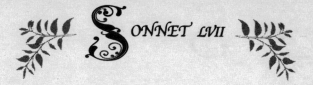

# SONNET LVII

Being your slave, what should I do but tend
Upon the hours and times of your desire?
I have no precious time at all to spend,
Nor services to do, till you require.
Nor dare I chide the world-without-end hour
Whilst I, my sovereign, watch the clock for you,
Nor think the bitterness of absence sour
When you have bid your servant once adieu.
Nor dare I question with my jealous thought
Where you may be, or your affairs suppose,
But, like a sad slave, stay and think of nought
Save, where you are how happy you make those.
   So true a fool is love that in your will,
   Though you do any thing, he thinks no ill.

# Sonnet LXXI

No longer mourn for me when I am dead

Than you shall hear the surly sullen bell

Give warning to the world that I am fled

From this vile world, with vilest worms to dwell.

Nay, if you read this line, remember not

The hand that writ it; for I love you so

That I in your sweet thoughts would be forgot,

If thinking on me then should make you woe.

O, if, I say, you look upon this verse

When I perhaps compounded am with clay,

Do not so much as my poor name rehearse,

But let your love even with my life decay,

    Lest the wise world should look into your moan

    And mock you with me after I am gone.

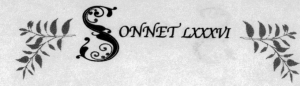

Was it the proud full sail of his great verse,

Bound for the prize of all too precious you,

That did my ripe thoughts in my brain inhearse,

Making their tomb the womb wherein they grew?

Was it his spirit, by spirits taught to write

Above a mortal pitch, that struck me dead?

No, neither he, nor his compeers by night

Giving him aid, my verse astonished.

He, nor that affable familiar ghost

Which nightly gulls him with intelligence,

As victors, of my silence cannot boast;

I was not sick of any fear from thence:

    But when your countenance filled up his line,

    Then lacked I matter; that enfeebled mine.

# SONNET XCVIII

From you have I been absent in the spring,

When proud-pied April, dressed in all his trim,

Hath put a spirit of youth in every thing,

That heavy Saturn laughed and leaped with him.

Yet nor the lays of birds, nor the sweet smell

Of different flowers in odour and in hue,

Could make me any summer's story tell,

Or from their proud lap pluck them where they grew:

Nor did I wonder at the lily's white,

Nor praise the deep vermilion in the rose;

They were but sweet, but figures of delight,

Drawn after you, you pattern of all those.

    Yet seemed it winter still, and, you away,

    As with your shadow I with these did play.

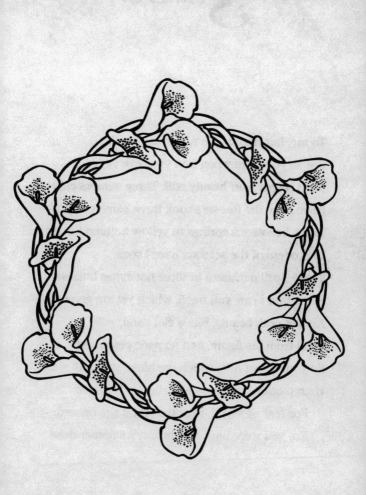

# SONNET CIV

To me, fair friend, you never can be old,

For as you were when first your eye I eyed,

Such seems your beauty still. Three winters cold

Have from the forests shook three summers' pride,

Three beauteous springs to yellow autumn turned

In process of the seasons have I seen,

Three April perfumes in three hot Junes burned,

Since first I saw you fresh, which yet are green.

Ah! yet doth beauty, like a dial hand,

Steal from his figure, and no pace perceived;

So your sweet hue, which methinks still doth stand,

Hath motion, and mine eye may be deceived;

   For fear of which, hear this, thou age unbred:

   Ere you were born was beauty's summer dead.

# SONNET CVI

When in the chronicle of wasted time
I see descriptions of the fairest wights,
And beauty making beautiful old rhyme
In praise of ladies dead and lovely knights,
Then, in the blazon of sweet beauty's best,
Of hand, of foot, of lip, of eye, of brow,
I see their antique pen would have expressed
Even such a beauty as you master now.
So all their praises are but prophecies
Of this our time, all you prefiguring;
And, for they looked but with divining eyes,
They had not skill enough your worth to sing:
    For we, which now behold these present days,
      Have eyes to wonder, but lack tongues to praise.

# SONNET CXVI

Let me not to the marriage of true minds
Admit impediments. Love is not love
Which alters when it alteration finds,
Or bends with the remover to remove.
O, no! it is an ever-fixed mark
That looks on tempests and is never shaken;
It is the star to every wandering bark,
Whose worth's unknown, although his height be taken.
Love's not Time's fool, though rosy lips and cheeks
Within his bending sickle's compass come;
Love alters not with his brief hours and weeks,
But bears it out even to the edge of doom.
   If this be error, and upon me proved,
   I never writ, nor no man ever loved.

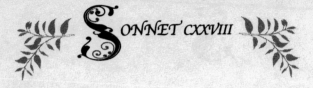

# SONNET CXXVIII

How oft, when thou, my music, music play'st,

Upon that blessed wood whose motion sounds

With thy sweet fingers, when thou gently sway'st

The wiry concord that mine ear confounds,

Do I envy those jacks that nimble leap

To kiss the tender inward of thy hand,

Whilst my poor lips, which should that harvest reap,

At the wood's boldness by thee blushing stand!

To be so tickled, they would change their state

And situation with those dancing chips,

O'er whom thy fingers walk with gentle gait,

Making dead wood more blest than living lips.

    Since saucy jacks so happy are in this,

    Give them thy fingers, me thy lips to kiss.

# SONNET CXXX

My mistress' eyes are nothing like the sun;

Coral is far more red than her lips' red;

If snow be white, why then her breasts are dun;

If hairs be wires, black wires grow on her head.

I have seen roses damasked, red and white,

But no such roses see I in her cheeks;

And in some perfumes is there more delight

Than in the breath that from my mistress reeks.

I love to hear her speak, yet well I know

That music hath a far more pleasing sound:

I grant I never saw a goddess go;

My mistress, when she walks, treads on the ground.

   And yet, by heaven, I think my love as rare

   As any she belied with false compare.

# SONNET CXXXVIII

When my love swears that she is made of truth
I do believe her, though I know she lies,
That she might think me some untutored youth,
Unlearned in the world's false subtleties.
Thus vainly thinking that she thinks me young,
Although she knows my days are past the best,
Simply I credit her false-speaking tongue:
On both sides thus is simple truth suppressed.
But wherefore says she not she is unjust?
And wherefore say not I that I am old?
O, love's best habit is in seeming trust,
And age in love loves not to have years told.
    Therefore I lie with her and she with me,
    And in our faults by lies we flattered be.

Live with me, and be my love,
And we will all the pleasures prove
That hills and valleys, dales and fields,
And all the craggy mountains yields.

There will we sit upon the rocks,
And see the shepherds feed their flocks,
By shallow rivers, by whose falls
Melodious birds sing madrigals.

There will I make thee a bed of roses,
With a thousand fragrant posies,
A cap of flowers, and a kirtle
Embroidered all with leaves of myrtle.

A belt of straw and ivy buds,
With coral clasps and amber studs;
And if these pleasures may thee move,
Then live with me and be my love.

## LOVE'S ANSWER

If that the world and love were young,
And truth in every shepherd's tongue,
These pretty pleasures might me move
To live with thee and be thy love.

*Sonnets to Sundry Notes of Music* (V)

# SONGS & POEMS

## FROM THE PLAYS

O mistress mine, where are you roaming?
O, stay and hear; your true love's coming,
    That can sing both high and low.
Trip no further, pretty sweeting;
Journeys end in lovers meeting,
    Every wise man's son doth know.

What is love? 'tis not hereafter;
Present mirth hath present laughter;
    What's to come is still unsure:
In delay there lies no plenty;
Then come kiss me, sweet and twenty,
    Youth's a stuff will not endure.


*Twelfth Night* (II, iii)

Who is Silvia? what is she,
    That all our swains commend her?
Holy, fair, and wise is she;
    The heaven such grace did lend her,
That she might admired be.

Is she kind as she is fair?
    For beauty lives with kindness.
Love doth to her eyes repair,
    To help him of his blindness,
And, being helped, inhabits there.

Then to Silvia let us sing,
    That Silvia is excelling;
She excels each mortal thing
    Upon the dull earth dwelling:
To her let us garlands bring.

*The Two Gentlemen of Verona* (IV, ii)

Sigh no more, ladies, sigh no more,
   Men were deceivers ever,
One foot in sea and one on shore,
   To one thing constant never.
Then sigh not so, but let them go,
   And be you blithe and bonny,
Converting all your sounds of woe
   Into Hey nonny, nonny.

Sing no more ditties, sing no moe,
   Of dumps so dull and heavy;
The fraud of men was ever so,
   Since summer first was leavy.

*Much Ado About Nothing* (II, iii)

Take, O, take those lips away,
      That so sweetly were forsworn;
And those eyes, the break of day,
   Lights that do mislead the morn:
But my kisses bring again, bring again;
Seals of love, but sealed in vain, sealed in vain.


*Measure for Measure* (IV, i)

Hark, hark! the lark at heaven's gate sings,
   And Phoebus 'gins arise,
His steeds to water at those springs
   On chaliced flowers that lies;
And winking Mary-buds begin
   To ope their golden eyes.
With every thing that pretty is,
   My lady sweet, arise:
      Arise, arise!

*Cymbeline* (II, iii)

t was a lover and his lass,
    With a hey, and a ho, and a hey nonino,
That o'er the green cornfield did pass
    In the springtime, the only pretty ring time,
When birds do sing, hey ding a ding, ding:
Sweet lovers love the spring.

Between the acres of the rye,
    With a hey, and a ho, and a hey nonino,
These pretty country folks would lie
    In the springtime, the only pretty ring time,
When birds do sing, hey ding a ding, ding:
Sweet lovers love the spring.

This carol they began that hour,
    With a hey, and a ho, and a hey nonino,
How that a life was but a flower
    In the springtime, the only pretty ring time,
When birds do sing, hey ding a ding, ding:
Sweet lovers love the spring.

And therefore take the present time,
    With a hey, and a ho, and a hey nonino,
For love is crowned with the prime
    In the springtime, the only pretty ring time,
When birds do sing, hey ding a ding, ding:
Sweet lovers love the spring.

*As You Like It* (V, iii)

So sweet a kiss the golden sun gives not
　　　To those fresh morning drops upon the rose,
As thy eye-beams when their fresh rays have smote
　　The night of dew that on my cheeks down flows.
Nor shines the silver moon one half so bright
　　Through the transparent bosom of the deep,
As doth thy face through tears of mine give light;
　　Thou shinest in every tear that I do weep.
No drop but as a coach doth carry thee;
　　So ridest thou triumphing in my woe.
Do but behold the tears that swell in me,
　　And they thy glory through my grief will show.
But do not love thyself; then thou wilt keep
My tears for glasses and still make me weep.
O queen of queens! how far dost thou excel
No thought can think, nor tongue of mortal tell.

*Love's Labour's Lost* (IV, iii)

Orpheus with his lute made trees,
And the mountain tops that freeze,
Bow themselves when he did sing.
To his music plants and flowers
Ever sprung, as sun and showers
There had made a lasting spring.

Every thing that heard him play,
Even the billows of the sea,
Hung their heads, and then lay by.
In sweet music is such art,
Killing care and grief of heart
Fall asleep, or hearing die.

*Henry VIII* (III, i)

# Index of First Lines

# I WAS AN OVERCOMMITTED CHRISTIAN

# I WAS AN OVER COMMITTED CHRISTIAN

by Nyla Jane Witmore

Tyndale House
Publishers, Inc.
Wheaton, Illinois

Library of Congress
Catalog Card Number
78-68908.
ISBN 0-8423-1585-3,
paper.
Copyright © 1979 by
Nyla Jane Witmore.
All rights reserved.
First printing, August
1979.
Printed in the United
States of America.

To "Joni," whose life story compelled me to do something with my life. . .

To Sue, Mary Loraine, and Gail, whose encouragement caused me to develop as a person and writer. . .

And especially to my beloved Jerry, whose nurturing and abiding love has caused me to see more of the Lord in our lives. . . .

# CONTENTS

*Introduction*

A few years ago I walked into a book store hoping to find a pamphlet or tract written for the tired, exhausted Christian.

The shelves were bulging with How-To texts on everything from how to find God, to inspirational pieces motivating the reader to rush eagerly to attempt even more for the cause of the Gospel.

I was already eyebrow deep in church activities, and loved every minute of it. Had I another head, two additional arms and legs, I'd have attempted even more.

After all, in a small church a few persons must be spread over a variety of services. Still there were the starving, lost, orphaned, and elderly to consider. Sound familiar?

There I stood staring at the shelves, wondering if anyone had written a book on Lifestyle Stewardship . . . the whys and wherefores of getting things done without burning-out or having a nervous breakdown.

Sorry to say, I never found a text that day. As a result, my life treadmilled through the months and years ahead. Exhaustion and fatigue occurred despite my daily discipline of a "quiet time" for prayer and Bible study.

Time revealed a moment of truth, as you will see in the coming chapters. I found myself living the pages of my own book.

Perhaps you too are standing in a book store wondering "Can I keep up the pace?" "Am I overcommitted or overworked?" "How can I plan for balance in my lifestyle?" "How concerned and involved is God in this process?"

I pray you will not have to experience a "burn-out" before discovering balance. Perhaps this book will help.

# ONE
## *First Clues: Early Symptoms of Over- commitment*

"I'm sorry, I can't check your homework. I've got a Sunday school teacher's meeting to attend." Grabbing my coat and hurrying toward the door, I turned to make one last parental pronouncement. "Your father will have to take care of it before family devotions tonight." I left for my meeting, leaving Jerry in charge.

Later that evening, I slipped quietly into the house. The lights were all out, except for the night light in the hall. I tiptoed quietly to the master bedroom. The fluorescent hands on the alarm clock marked exactly 11:00 P.M.

All was still, except for the quiet breathing sounds of my husband, our two young boys, and the miniature poodle who slept in the hallway.

Why did so many evenings seem to end this way? I was beginning to feel cheated. We never had time together anymore. Every evening was simply more of the same—meetings, meetings, meetings.

As I crept quietly beneath the sheets, Jerry stirred. Surely he deserved more than this, I thought. I had the aching feeling I had missed something along the way.

When did things start to get so rushed and demanding? I sensed we couldn't go on like this.

Turning over, I said my prayers silently. Then, plumping limp pillows, I wearily settled in for the night.

That night, I had no way of knowing the days and year ahead would become so full of confusion, resentment, and guilt. For the first time in my life, I was about to see what over-commitment could do to one's mental, physical, emotional, and spiritual well-being.

The next morning I was still bothered by an uneasy feeling.

While fixing the dry cereal and juice, I thought about last night's meeting. I liked going to meetings at church. There was something magnetic about the building, the pastor, and the people. Even the lingering meetings in which little was accomplished seemed to hold something for me I couldn't find in the secular world.

"I love the people at church," I thought as I poured the orange juice. "It's a privilege to be with them, not a burden. Face it, Nyla, you love church work."

But I loved my family too, and it was beginning to look as if I couldn't have both.

I set out the cereal bowls at each place setting and hoped I hadn't forgotten anything.

Deeply lost in thought, I wondered, "Why is it, in the labyrinth of doing God's work, that things get dim and out of focus at times? Goals once set to put family first just fade into a blur of quick meals, hasty homework, and brief times of close conversation."

13

I poured the juice in each glass. "This morning is no different," I said under my breath.

Putting out the milk and sugar, I suddenly remembered I'd forgotten the napkins again, my usual error. "You'd think I'd learn when it's the same item I forget every day." I pulled four paper napkins from the drawer.

"Tomorrow I'll get organized," I promised myself.

I called Jerry and the children to breakfast.

"Tomorrow I'll get organized."

# TWO
## *The Rationalizing Phase*

With Jerry off to work and the breakfast dishes still sitting in the sink, the phone began its faithful ringing.

I knew this day would be the same as the rest—a hurried visit with a friend via the phone, followed by a rushed gathering of children's toys and a hasty comb through my hair. As soon as everyone was dressed, we'd be out the door heading for a neighborhood Bible study or prayer group. Sometimes I visited church friends in order that our children might have companionship.

Emotionally and spiritually I felt

house-bound. Meetings meant stimulating conversation beyond the challenges of pat-a-cake and waving "bye-bye."

The phone became my most welcomed intruder. I rationalized that I could still be home dusting and whisk-brooming my way through life, all the while resolving spiritual and childrearing philosophies.

The challenge of doing two or three things at once was expected—even normal—for a mother with young children.

I recall one afternoon spent juggling a phone at my ear, a spoon in my hand, and a whining four-year-old tugging at my hem.

"Excuse me, Sue," I stirred the pot with my big spoon. "Let me get more comfortable while we talk. I'll put the soup on simmer and play with Chris while keeping an eye on the stove."

We talked for what seemed just a few minutes. Chris soon became impatient with a pull-toy. I crooked my neck to hold the phone in place between my ear and shoulder. "Let me see if I can fix it for you, honey."

By now he was looking distraught, impatient with my efforts to extricate the pull-string from the wheels. Perhaps he was simply annoyed with my attachment to the black thing I held in the crook of my neck.

The whining started. "Wait, dear. Mommy will find you a snack or something." By now he was stamping his feet to accompany his wailing.

The cookie quickly disappeared, leaving crusty tidbits everywhere. "Here, play with these plastic cups." My hands raced to find another diversion in order that I might continue my conversation without further interruption.

All the while, Sue and I talked about church things, the things we didn't understand in the Bible, and the things God was doing in our lives. It was a rich time of sharing punctuated by the little interruptions of mothering.

I began building towers and castles with the plastic shapes. Chris gleefully pushed them over.

At the end of the conversation I faced a wet-legged youngster and a million crumbs scattered over the entire house.

What did I learn from this? Only that mothers are destined to be domestic octopuses. I had learned to do six, seven, or eleven jobs in tandem. They weren't all done well, mind you, but at least I attempted.

I responded to the most immediate cry for help. Jerry said I was operating in "interrupt mode." Is that what it's called? I thought I was just losing my mind. Does everyone live this way?

# THREE
## *The How-Did-I-Get-Here? Phase*

Invariably the human animal looks for reasons for failures. I was no exception. I had lived through the rationalizing and justifying stages. The more I struggled, the deeper I sank in the quicksand I was making for myself.

Where had this voracious appetite for activity come from? The puritanical work ethic? The frantic pace of TV? Hyperactivity caused by junk foods and refined sugar?

I couldn't find the answer from outside myself. The truth was, the answer originated from within—from a renewed awakening of my commitment to Christ the year before. I was still riding high on the honeymoon phase of my new relationship with Jesus. My appetite for just one more prayer group, Bible study, or famous speaker seemed insatiable.

"I just don't understand your striving, Nyla." Jerry didn't know what to make of my round-the-clock quest for spiritual knowledge, but he lovingly bore with me.

When friends began to comment, "Nyla, don't you think you're doing too much?" I quickly tossed their remarks aside. "No, I can handle it," I'd reply. "Besides, somebody's got to do it."

I should have known I was over-committed when I misplaced my keys three times in one day. Sometimes I found normal things in abnormal places . . . like the time I opened my cupboard to find the milk quietly curdling next to the canned goods.

Then I suffered with shingles plus a two-month case of raging poison ivy. Even my usual clumsiness was worse than ever. My body was trying to tell me something.

When the gentle and not-so-gentle nudgings from friends became more frequent, I began to wonder if the "witness of two or three" was divinely ordained to make me stop for a second look at my life.

"Seek ye *first* (italics added) the Kingdom of God . . ." (Matt. 6:33). Surely I must be doing the right thing, I thought. It was God's work, and I was doing it *first*.

Somewhere along the way, "Seek ye first the Kingdom of God" had become "*Seek ye only* the Kingdom of God."

I hadn't noticed this fact until one evening at dinner. After I had given a fifteen-minute nonstop discourse on the church's latest problems and projects, my husband interrupted. "Nyla, isn't there anything else we can talk about besides church?"

I was hurt, defensive, enraged. And yet I had to admit that besides church friends, I had only passing acquaintances. Community involvement? None, unless you count weekly grocery shopping. Neighbors? I waved and honked as I passed them on my way to prayer groups and Bible studies.

I was proud that I watched so little TV. Would that I could have dropped little tidbits gleaned from morning news programs to spice up the evening's conversations. But I'd used up most of that time on other things.

I could have explored all those areas, but I didn't. Next to the things of God, they were mundane and boring. The work of the church was exciting and alive! There weren't enough hours in the day to get involved with the rest of the world, I reasoned.

Finally my husband took me aside. "Do you think we could sit down some evening and talk about our use of time?"

Secretly I wanted to reply, "Well, if I *have* the time." But I knew the discussion was necessary, so I agreed.

As we finished sipping our after-dinner tea, he began to tell me more—the concerns he had for our future.

# FOUR
## *The Visualizing Phase*

"I'm not trying to tell you how to live your life," Jerry said. "It just seems that both of us are spending our lives in only one or two areas."

I appreciated his candor. Once I moved beyond initial defensiveness, I felt a sense of relief. He cared where our lives were heading.

Walking toward our large family wall calendar, already crowded with commitments, he scratched his chin thoughtfully. "Hmmmm, this gives me an idea." Then, removing two of the used sheets, he turned and said, "Why don't we use these to mark down a full month's activities?"

Handing me a pencil he said, "You mark yours and then we'll compare."

"What shall we look for?" I wanted to know.

"It seems that most of our commitments should fall into three basic categories: daily, weekly, or monthly. Fill in all the regular daily things first; then do the weekly, and so on."

I groaned, but knew he made sense. Then it occurred to me that the activities probably fell into topical areas as well. "Maybe we should consider some generalized groupings of activity." My creative juices were flowing with the challenge of using my mind for something other than menu planning. "Why not include things like religious activity, family-centered times, household and domestic. . . ."

"I'd better change that last category to 'job-related' on my chart," Jerry interrupted. "There aren't that many fix-it jobs in an average day for me."

"Oh, maybe we should include a category for physical exercise and leisure. That would be fourth on our chart."

With our plan of attack mapped

out, we sat down to have a quiet time with our calendars.

After making the first few entries, I stood back for a quick review. It was amazing how quickly those once-a-month entries were adding up.

Committee members or friends would approach me with projects: some challenging, some "blah" but necessary. "It won't take much of your time, Nyla. It's *only* once a month."

I echoed their reasoning at the time, convincing myself that surely anyone could manage a once-a-month commitment. Besides, I wanted to do some of these things. If the project was stimulating and God-oriented, how could it be wrong?

I pulled my thoughts back to the task of marking my calendar. "What commitments are daily at this point?" I wondered. I wrote down regular prayer and personal devotions. For the most part I was well disciplined in that area.

I spent little time in personal grooming. Wash-and-wear fabrics eliminated most of my ironing chores,

and my basket of to-be-mended items
was full and dusty.

Weekly grooming tasks were a low
priority. Sporadically I'd consider
giving myself a manicure, but usually
my nails appeared torn and worn. I
reasoned, "I'll do only those things
that have to be done."

Colognes that Jerry had given me a
year before sat untouched on the
bathroom shelves. Jerry liked me to
wear fragrances. He'd told me so on
several occasions. I never seemed to
remember unless we were going out
for dinner.

Some things I didn't forget, such as
the Bible studies, prayer groups,
teacher's training at church,
evangelism training classes, and
nursing home visitations.

My calendar seemed to be getting
full.

I laughed when I looked at the
domestic duties I'd listed (splotchy,
half-completed, and halfhearted).

"Good thing I don't have to record
phone interruptions," I thought. The
impossibility of charting such diver-

sions was beginning to cause me to leave suspicious blanks of unaccounted time on the calendar. How would I explain so much wasted time?

Ah, the phone. Such a marvelous invention. The phone's ringing at that moment would have been a welcome break from my work sheet.

While some persons might have had cravings for cigarettes or black coffee, I had phone cravings. I had a similar weakness for cookies and sweets.

Suddenly I broke the studious silence. "Honey, I think I hear a cookie calling me. How about you?" I hoped Jerry would jump at the chance for a snack break. He put down his pen, raided the cookie jar for both of us, then went back to work.

With my chewing diversions completed, I too returned to the task of charting.

Looking at the crumbs on my lap I was reminded of other cleaning chores. "Heaven forbid that anyone should see the inside of my closets and drawers!"

Drawers and cupboards represented

the hidden clutter of my life. I would someday come to see the state of my drawers as a gauge of the balance or imbalance between the secular and spiritual areas of my life.

Then on to family-centered activity. I wished I could count family mealtimes. Dinner hours fluctuated due to Jerry's erratic working hours. Having one car promoted family solidarity in one sense, but it provided fuel for disorganization in other ways.

For example, the children were normally starving by 5:00 P.M. Truthfully, I was ravenous at 4:00, and by the time 6:00 rolled by, my blood sugar had dipped enough to render me less than coherent. We solved that. I started feeding the children and myself at 5:00. Then the rest of us joined Daddy at dinner for the dessert. But sharing dessert together wasn't like sharing a whole meal.

I marked down the meal hours but left the classification blank. Then on to TV time.

"How do I classify TV? We so seldom talk during the reruns of 'The Partridge Family' and 'I Love Lucy,' " I mumbled to myself. I could still hear someone saying, "Get down in front, you're blocking my view." At other times I could recall orchestrated *"Shhhhhhhhs"* filling the air. I could see I was getting nowhere.

"Surely we have more family times than these," I thought. My pencil began tapping nervously on the kitchen table.

"You're tapping rhythms again, Nyla." Jerry's voice sounded irritated. "I can't think when you do that."

"Sorry," I said. "I forget what I'm doing."

I would have counted movies as my next item under "Family," but I realized that the only talking at those times was for the purpose of taking orders for popcorn and soft drinks.

Riding to church fell into the same category. We usually rushed out the door still combing hair and adjusting belt buckles. By the time the last hair was in place, we were usually pulling into the church's parking lot.

As for church, with Jerry and me teaching separate classes, we only saw each other in the pew at 11:00. That nixed my plans for counting church as both a religious and a family activity. In fact, the chaos that ensued each Lord's day almost tempted me to disqualify it from both categories.

Between church and Sunday school the children ran wild, chased paper airplanes they'd made in the nursery, threw pebbles in the parking lot (at the pastor's car!), and ran in and out of the bathrooms with the frequency of a woman in her ninth month of pregnancy. Controlling the children's adrenaline was not a top priority. We selfishly but naturally yearned to have some adult fellowship on Sunday morning. Teaching Sunday school didn't give us that opportunity, so we lingered between and after services to catch up on socializing.

Enough reflection on family life. It was getting depressing.

I looked up from my last entry. Jerry was working intently on his chart. His pen moved swiftly across the graph of daily squares. Would that my pencil could move with such precision! Perhaps that was part of my problem. I never finished anything completely. Thoroughness was not one of my assets.

"Got your categories finished?" Jerry asked as he put the final touches on his orderly masterpiece.

"Just about; I only have the 'physical exercise' list to do." I pretended to be deep in thought. "It shouldn't take long."

How right I was. I couldn't think of any physical activity except shoveling us out of six snowstorms last winter. We snow skied and water-skied a total of ten days last year. So much for skiing. For summer, the swims in the pool usually degenerated into tanning oil massages. And except for an occasional skating lesson with a local mothers' class, there wasn't much in the way of regular muscle development. My only hope was to count vacuuming and dusting as both domestic and physical activity.

"Isn't physical activity supposed to be enjoyable?" I mumbled aloud.

Jerry looked up amused. "I can

think of a couple of physical things I enjoy doing with you. They are both definitely enjoyable!" His eyes twinkled.

One was easy to figure, the second not so easy. "What do you mean?" I inquired. Jerry chewed thoughtfully on the tip of his pen, then replied "Well, I enjoyed skating with you last winter. Maybe we should take up something together. What do you think?"

"That might not be a bad idea," I offered. "Maybe something will come out of all this besides the writer's cramp I'm developing in my index finger." A glimmer of optimism was beginning to surface.

I looked up at the clock. It had been only ten or fifteen minutes at the most since we had begun.

I was beginning to learn a valuable truth: *Threatening and unpleasant tasks take so little time once we force ourselves to get started.*

An artistic urge struck me at that moment. What would happen if we color-coded those calendar entries?

I rustled through one of my "Fibber Magee" drawers to find a set of light-colored felt pens. Having once read a book on time and motion studies (the "how-to-do-three-things-at-once" books), I figured I'd save recopying efforts. By coloring each category with a different color, the areas of greatest participation could be seen at a glance. I beamed at my brilliance.

Handing Jerry a yellow pen, I offered a suggestion. "Let's use this one for all our spiritual activities." I watched as Jerry marked over the writing on his calendar: weekly—Sunday school teacher; monthly—elders' meeting, church council session, teachers' meeting, planning boards; occasional—a church roof repair project.

Turning attention to my own list, I cringed at the ominous possibility that when I finished, I'd have a totally yellow page staring back at me. I proceeded speechless, hoping my suspicions would be unfounded.

But even after color-coding the remaining three categories, a quick glance revealed at least 80 percent of my waking hours were spent in religious or spiritual endeavors.

"Well," I asked, "where do we go from here?"

# FIVE
## *The Wrenching Transition Phase*

"I don't think we can make hasty decisions, Nyla."

Decisions? I was in no condition to decide anything . . . hastily or otherwise.

Before anything in our lifestyles could be changed or altered, we knew the first task must be to determine priorities.

"Priorities," I blurted. "If I knew how to set priorities, I wouldn't be in this mess."

I was tempted to read off my list of "musts" right then. I wanted to say, "I've got to continue this activity and that one, too. I can't let those people down."

But I recalled another time when I had read off my list of conflicts in decision making. Jerry had said, "Well, I see we're playing 'ain't it awful' again."

I had to admit the same element would have been true this day as well. Certain traditions and rituals had become so ingrained in our lives over the years that my decisions were bound to be influenced by them. I shuddered.

"Shall we discuss it after dinner?"

"Sure, that's the best time." Now we were being practical.

After the children were tucked in bed, I edged closer to Jerry.

"Ready to talk now, honey?"

"Sure."

He put his paper on the coffee table, plumped some pillows on the couch, and we began to talk.

What seemed an orderly, mature, and unemotional beginning ended two hours later in tears and frustration.

It was clear this was not going to be

as easy as a few scribbles on an old calendar.

Inside, I was screaming: "Something's got to give, but does it have to be me?"

I was frustrated, and this was only the beginning!

A few weeks and many discussions later . . .

"I can't give up anything I'm doing now." My voice sounded adamant. "They're counting on me. Besides, the church is small and there aren't enough people to take on the work that needs doing."

For the next hour we discussed item by item the entries on my calendar chart. Jerry insisted the decisions would have to be mine.

His nondirective approach was best, though I could not see it at the time. What I wanted most was someone to wield a surgeon's knife to my problems.

"I believe God can use me as a teacher. I want to be a teacher. Why would God give me a gift of teaching and then ask me not to use it? God wouldn't do that."

All I could think of was disappointing God's people, or God himself. It felt like a divorce!

Summer was coming. "I'll finish directing the vacation Bible school . . . they couldn't get anyone else. Then I'll think about slowing down."

What I hadn't counted on was the degree of exhaustion to which I was subjecting my already fatigued body. My spiritual storehouses were being emptied faster than they were being refilled.

This was the first time I'd faced squarely the prospects of altering my Christian service roster. It wouldn't be the last.

As the days and weeks passed, I spent more time seeking God's will in the matter of Christian stewardship.

I'd hear myself cry, "I just want to know you're still in control, Lord." I needed assurances. Then I began to pray more honestly, "I don't mind your changing my gifts and talents —or even taking some away. Just let me know I'm where *you* want me."

I talked to God regularly along those lines. Though I never heard a voice talk back I would sense he loved me.

I began to notice his loving me through the Scriptures. More and more I would read Scriptures that seemed to shout from the pages.

One such time I was drawn to the example of Abraham. I began thinking of his struggle to give up something he loved best. I wondered if God was going to require a sacrifice of me as well.

Then the word "idolatry" came into the picture—not the statues or graven images one normally thinks of when reviewing the Ten Commandments —rather, the kind of daily idolatry that results when anything becomes too important, or more important than God would like.

I began to ask, *"Has my Christian work become more important than listening for the changes and cancellations the Lord might want to direct?"*

Another word kept cropping up— "Reroute." I thought of Jonah, rerouted by a fish. How could God reroute me, if I strayed from the center of his plans? I wondered.

A few weeks later God allowed me to see each of these words come together in a meaningful whole. It was as though he permitted each word to incubate sufficiently before allowing me to experience the hatching.

We were vacationing on the Cape, which to anyone outside New England is translated Cape Cod. While attending services one Sunday in East Dennis I heard a pastor say: "If it takes you considerable struggling before you can be rerouted by God—maybe you're having an idolatrous relationship with something." Ouch!

As I thought about that sermon I began to open some private closets in my thinking. "Am I really clinging to talents and gifts solely on the basis that they are for the Lord's work and therefore right?" I had casually considered such prospects before, but never with such honesty as now.

Two rather startling thoughts came to mind:

1. What if God might be desiring to develop a new talent or gift in me? By learning to be idle for a time, I might develop "listening ears" to God's direction. (That was how Jonah learned.)
2. Was God testing my willingness to give up certain activities and gifts,

in order that he might renew and empower that same gift at a later time? (After all, God returned Abraham's son to him after Abraham showed willingness to let go.)

Had I finally reached my moment of truth? Would I experience idleness and a sacrificial letting-go?

A few months later I experienced both. We moved and we found a new church home. For a year we experienced a long overdue sabbatical rest.

I felt guilty about not rushing to enter the arena of "organized" Christian service, until I came across a passage in Hebrews 4:9, 10 (RSV).

"There remains a sabbath rest for the people of God; for whoever enters God's rest also *ceases from his labors* as God did from his."

If God took a rest from godly functions . . . so could I!

# SEVEN
## *Healing Places*

From the pulpit one Sunday we heard these words: "If I see you too many nights in a row at church, I'm going to tell you you're doing too much . . . go home to your family."

"Hallelujah," I said quietly under my breath.

As our family drove home from church, I commented to Jerry, "I get the feeling that our pastor cares about balance." He quickly agreed.

The spring air felt good as we rolled down windows for an extra rush of sweet fragrance. The apple trees in full bloom provided splashes of blinding whiteness against the New England countryside.

"I feel like those trees—free to bloom," I said. "Isn't it good *not* to feel spiritually muscle-bound anymore?" Jerry nodded in assent.

We drove some time, viewing the countryside which had now become so familiar. As I admired the rolling New England farmlands, I found myself thinking about the natural rock fences crisscrossing the panorama.

"God gave us a natural fence too . . ." I heard myself saying.

"Hmmmm, what do you mean?" Jerry asked, puzzled by my comparison.

"Well, I think God gave us a natural fence too. It's the family."

The word *family* had become so much more meaningful in the last year. Even the children seemed happier.

"I'll bet you'll be surprised to know that I haven't missed the phone's ringing." I looked over quickly to catch his reaction.

Jerry smiled one of those knowing

smiles. "I thought you'd like it once you got used to it."

I reached out to touch his sleeve. "Jerry, in the past year I've learned to depend on *you* instead of friends. You've become my very best friend!"

I don't know whether the heaving chest I saw in the driver's seat was a sigh of relief or of pride. It didn't matter.

"I think I've learned something else lately. . . . I'm actually enjoying the boys in ways I never thought possible."

Our two sons beamed in the back seat. They knew we were happy. It made them happy too.

Even family devotions had taken a turn for the better in recent months. These regular and frequent quiet times as a family had launched Jerry as the true spiritual leader of our family.

"Why does it take so long to discover that family life means so much?"

Such a question hardly needed answering. The answer was supplied as our lives approached the priorities God wanted us to have, rather than the selfish, self-serving motives that seemed so attractive and right to us at the time.

What indeed would God choose for us? We were just beginning to find out.

# EIGHT
## *Rehabilitation and Reentry*

How does one begin again when the sabbatical is over? Finding out was the next step.

"What will I do when I'm asked to serve and volunteer again?" I asked Jerry.

He reminded me that an undisciplined reentry would not serve God's purpose.

I knew it too. But I was concerned others would not understand my reason for being slow to volunteer.

Would I have the courage to tell others I was recovering from a case of spiritual exhaustion?

I wasn't "Super Christian," "Wonder Woman," or even the "Bionic Blonde." I had learned that the hard way. And now I would have to admit it again, every time some stimulating and exciting task tempted me.

I promised myself, "If it doesn't fit in with the overall balance of our devotional and family life, it isn't right for me to do."

That philosophy would, of course, force me to look at the needs and desires of our *entire* family before making additional commitments.

I recalled a time recorded in Scripture when "each man did what was pleasing in his own eyes" (see Deut. 12:8). I didn't want to be guilty of repeating that.

I thought about the gifts and talents God had given Jerry. There would be times when I would need to change some of my plans so that he might exercise his abilities for the church and community.

Then I thought about the developing gifts and abilities of our two sons. They were still young, but we needed to teach an attitude of balanced stewardship in their formative years.

At this point in our lives it seemed unfair to share our gifts only with believers. We would need to consider which gifts the Lord might want us to use to bless unbelievers as well.

Thus the prospects for a new stewardship of our lives, time, and talents loomed as both frightening and challenging.

## NINE
*My Yoke
Is Easy . . .*

The entire "break-down, burn-out,
and break-through" process took place
over a period of three or four years.

Those years were both the worst—
and the best.

I learned that *slow and steady*
growth has lasting potential; that it
isn't necessary for every Christian
experience and challenge to be solved
with an "instant" or "convenience-
food" theology.

Slow and steady—like cactus. They
grow slowly . . . they're supposed to.
And look how long they last! I wanted
desperately to last too.

But there's something else. I once

51

heard a friend use the expression—
"Don't pick up every bundle. Not every bundle has your name on it."

In past years I doubted that. Didn't Scripture tell us to "Bear ye one another's burdens . . ." (Gal. 6:2)? It was later I learned to bear only those burdens that bear my name. I learned to tell the difference. I can't carry them all.

Aha! It then became apparent why Nyla Witmore had burned herself out for the Lord. I had tried to do everything.

I must constantly remind myself today that God may choose someone else to bring the message of saving faith and renewal to one of my loved ones. Someone else may be chosen to be a stronger spiritual influence in the lives of my children. It may not be me.

So I take my hands off the temptation to "fix things" for everyone I meet. Everything doesn't depend on me.

My big concern today is this: How

do I know when I'm in a God-pleasing flow?

I sense it most when I am serving without strain or a nagging sense of pressure. I sense it when I am able to see a balanced calendar. I sense it when I'm home with the family more nights than I'm away. I sense it when I don't hear the children asking, "Who's the baby-sitter tonight?"

*In a myriad of ways my eyes can see*
*The manner of*
*Mother*
*Wife*
*And friend*
*I'm meant to be.*

For me, I must stop briefly and listen to the "still small voice" God provides to believers.

Then I see Jesus' words—"*My* yoke is easy . . . *My* burden is light." My eyes light up. Eureka! I understand it now.

God's loads (the bundles with *my* name on them) are light. He gives me just enough strength to handle those packages.

HOW do I know? Scripture tells me so: "No temptation has overtaken you that is not common to man. God is faithful, and he will not let you be tempted beyond your strength, but with the temptation will also provide the way of escape, that you may be able to endure it" (1 Cor. 10:13, RSV).

# TEN
*Slow . . .*
*Proceed with*
*Caution*

From the scars of past mistakes and
burn-outs, I developed a checklist to
help keep curbs on the use of my time
and talents.

SPIRITUAL CHECKLIST:
1. Are my priorities in order? God,
   husband, family, Christian and
   community service. Are there
   any weak spots at this time?
   Where?

2. Private Devotions: Did I sub-
   stitute public or family devotions in place of the intimate

one-on-one with the Lord today?
This week?

3. When I prayed, did I allow times
   of silence? Did I run through my
   prayer list and then run on
   about my own business? Did I
   try to hide from God, using the
   excuse, "I just didn't have time
   to even pray today"?

4. When asked to make a commitment for the church or community, did I try to avoid giving
   an immediate answer? Did I
   promise myself to pray during a
   given period of time *before* giving
   my answer?

5. If I had my mind partly made up
   when asked to participate, did I
   make known to God that I'd be
   willing to have *my* preferences
   changed or rerouted if *his* will so
   desired?

ATTITUDE CHECKLIST:
1. Do I think of myself more highly
   than I ought? "I bid every one

among you not to think of himself more highly than he ought. . ." (Rom. 12:3, RSV).

2. Am I willing to believe I can be expendable?

3. Am I keeping my eye peeled for pride when any activity or project might puff up my ego?

PHYSICAL CHECKLIST:
1. Do I have any physical symptoms that indicate I'm overextending myself (i.e. sickness, chronic run-down feelings, headaches without medical explanation, the desire to nap excessively)?

2. Do I have any vitamin deficiencies contributing to these feelings?

INTERPERSONAL CHECKLIST:
1. Do I find I'm unable to listen to an individual without allowing my thoughts and eyes to dart

around the room, as if I need or
want to be doing something else?

2. Am I persistently short-
tempered with loved ones?

THOUGHT-LIFE CHECKLIST:
1. Do I find I can't control my day-
dreaming?

2. Do certain thoughts consume my
waking hours and distract me
excessively when I try to go to
sleep at night?

CALENDAR CHECKLIST:
1. Are there any obvious imbal-
ances observable by checking my
calendar? (Consider that Little
League doesn't last forever;
likewise Christmas and Eas-
ter . . . don't be too hard on yourself if the crunch of activity will
be over soon.)

2. When was the last time I
checked my calendar *thoroughly*?
(Watch out . . . it sneaks up on
you.)

ACTION:

1. Maintain sense of humor at any cost.

2. Get rest!

3. Squeeze out five or ten minutes (it *is* possible) to lie down with pillows under your knees to relax each afternoon.

4. Change your daily pace by interspersing "surprises" (i.e., take your husband to lunch— be a mystery lunch guest on his business calendar; take a warm bath in the afternoon while sipping a cool beverage; buy a bouquet of flowers for yourself; visit a museum).

5. *Plan* a vacation . . . don't wait for one to happen. (Look forward to rest!)

6. Take a sabbatical rest (it's biblical).

7. When you see commitments are obviously excessive, set a two-week limit during which you will try to:

a. Delegate some jobs to others who need to develop gifts and talents in those areas where you are becoming "muscle-bound."
b. Eliminate those activities which are simply "wants" rather than "needs."
c. Maintain those activities that really cannot be done by someone else (i.e., nursing a baby!).

8. Be willing to work slowly. Instant solutions and hasty decisions often remove symptoms, but underlying causes remain to bubble up later.

9. Take credit as well as the blame when it is due. Stop playing "Adam," by blaming others for your failures.

10. After admitting infallibility is impossible, choose to get on with the business of living. *Stop looking back at past failures.* (That's a tough one.)

# ELEVEN
## A
## *Final*
## *Word*

Riding along through the beautiful countryside of rural New England, I see a sign: "Watch Out for Frost Heaves."

You see, our winters in Massachusetts are rugged and long. The effects of frost can be seen on the roadways as the snow begins to melt in March and April. Due to uneven freezing and thawing effects, small and large humps of asphalt appear to make the streets as rough as old-fashioned washboards.

The road crews are out each spring to make repairs, but heaves return every spring in old familiar places, as well as new ones.

My ride down the roadway to Christian stability and balance is much the same. Though I make my personal road repairs periodically, the "frost heaves" of overinvolvement and overcommitment still appear.

The difference today is the manner in which I face my "spiritual" frost heaves.

When Jerry and I made our discovery of imbalance, our roadway was so out of control that minor road repairs were impossible. We literally had to rip up some pavement and put down new asphalt. We couldn't travel much while the new roadway was being built.

Today we have a fresh road. Now we have the challenge of taking care of it. Road maintenance! That's where we're operating—guarding our health, our family, and our marriage with constructive jealousy.

Ah, I hear the phone ringing. "Yes . . . Jerry? You want me to pick you up from work? Love to. Be right there."

I open the cupboard nearest the sink, where I keep a hidden cache of perfume. A dab here, a dab there . . . I'm ready to go.

Now . . . if I can just find my keys!